THE FABER LIBRARY

OF ILLUMINATED MANUSCRIPTS

edited by Walter Oakeshott

The Vienna Genesis

THE FABER LIBRARY OF ILLUMINATED MANUSCRIPTS

edited by Walter Oakeshott

THE BENEDICTIONAL OF ST. ETHELWOLD
Francis Wormald

THE PARISIAN MINIATURIST HONORÉ
Eric Millar

THE GREAT LAMBETH BIBLE
C. R. Dodwell

THE ROHAN BOOK OF HOURS
Jean Porcher

THE VIENNA GENESIS
Emmy Wellesz

A FIFTEENTH CENTURY PLUTARCH
Charles Mitchell

THE
VIENNA GENESIS

with an introduction and notes

by

EMMY WELLESZ

FABER AND FABER LIMITED

24 Russell Square London

FIRST PUBLISHED IN MCMLX
BY FABER AND FABER LIMITED
24 RUSSELL SQUARE LONDON WCI
PRINTED IN GREAT BRITAIN
BY WESTERN PRINTING SERVICES, BRISTOL
COLOUR PLATES MADE BY PATZELT, VIENNA AND PRINTED
BY FINE ART ENGRAVERS, GUILDFORD

Introduction

The Vienna Genesis (Cod. Vindob. theol. graec. 31) was transferred to the Imperial Library in 1664. The Librarian who discovered the manuscript among the works of art left to the Emperor Leopold I by his uncle, that great collector and connoisseur, the Archduke Leopold Wilhelm, recognized at once its unique significance. He wrote to the Emperor: 'Exultavi pro gaudio ubi eximium hoc cimelium conspexi'—'I was transported with joy when I discovered this gem'. In fact, ever since it became known, the Vienna Genesis has been regarded as one of the outstanding manuscripts of all time. It has great aesthetic qualities: the fine uncial writing is done in silver on purple parchment, the lower half of each page being reserved for the painter. Script and paintings, together with the sumptuous background, form an admirable unity. Since most of the illustrations are in two superposed rows, the manuscript contains many more pictures than pages.

Apart from its appeal as a work of art, the Vienna Genesis is also outstanding as one of the main sources for the study of late classical book illustration in general and, in particular, of the beginnings of Bible illustration.

In order to realize how important it is in this respect, we must remember that it is one of two Greek illustrated Old Testament manuscripts, which alone have survived from pre-Iconoclastic times. The other is the Cotton Bible in the British Museum (Cod. Cotton Otho B.VI) attributed to the V Century A.D.[1] There is a similar scarcity of early Latin illustrated documents. Here, again, only two fragmentary Old Testament manuscripts have been left from pre-Carolingian days: the 'Quedlinburg Itala' in Berlin (State Library, Cod. theol. lat. fol. 485), and the 'Ashburnham Pentateuch' in Paris (Bibl. nat. nouv. acq. lat. 2334).

The Vienna Genesis is by far the richest and best preserved among all these fragments, Latin and Greek alike. It has therefore, since its discovery, been the subject of the most intensive research which has given rise to extremely violent controversy.

Before entering into the many questions involved we shall try to give a short description of the manuscript and of its paintings. The Vienna Genesis is of considerable size, consisting of forty-eight pages, which measure in length between 30.4–32.6 cm. and in width 24.5–26.5 cm. On the whole the text follows the Septuagint's first book of Moses, but it ranges only from the Fall of Man to Jacob's death. Apart from the fact that beginning and end are missing, there are considerable gaps in various other parts of the existing manuscript. Careful investigations have shown that originally the codex must have contained at least 96 pages with 192 illustrations. Since the great majority of the pictures is composed of several scenes, the complete number of scenes—or 'iconographic units'—has been estimated at 400–500.

A comparison of the surviving text with the analogous sections of the Septuagint shows that some passages were left out, others shortened and condensed, with the result that, with very few exceptions, each event, indeed every single phase of each event, which is told in words is also narrated in the pictures, these being sometimes even more explicit than the text. As Hans Gerstinger puts it in his comments to the facsimile edition,[2] 'In fact, our Genesis can hardly be called an illustrated Bible, but rather a Bible in pictures; not in the sense of the medieval *Biblia pauperum* or the typological *Bibles historiées*. It is an essentially historical, naïvely narrative biblical picture book.'

Two scribes were engaged in producing our copy; the first is responsible for folios I–XVI, the second for the remaining folios XVII–XXIV. Not only is there a difference in the writing itself, which is more ornamentally calligraphic in the first part, but also in the handling of the text.

The first scribe (Plates 1–6) attempts to give on each page a coherent story, an explicit caption, as it were, to the pictures below. To this end, apart from reducing his text in the way previously described, he sometimes leaves out unimportant words, uses smaller characters at the bottom of the allotted area, and occasionally leaves narrower spaces between the written lines. The second scribe (Plates 7–8) usually allows the text to flow continuously from one page to the other. In consequence, there is no need for him to have recourse to the first scribe's procedure of crowding the bottom of the script area. The first scribe's improvised fashion of fitting the writing into the script area has persuaded some scholars that the pictures were painted before the scribe started his work.

The surviving text starts with Genesis III, 4, and, accordingly, the first miniature shows the Fall of Man, the second the Expulsion from Paradise. Both are framed and they contain several scenes. Then follows the representation of the Flood (Plate 1). Together with one other in the first series of paintings, which illustrate the text written by the first scribe, this picture is exceptional in showing only one single scene. As the caption shows, it follows Genesis VII, 19–VIII, 13, but the lines about Noah sending out first a raven and then a dove, as well as the dove's return, have been omitted from the text, as their illustration has been from the picture.[3] The rectangular miniature with its painted background stands out distinctly against the purple of the page. The Flood is shown at its height: around the partly submerged ark, human beings and beasts, dead or in the last stages of their agony, are visible through the transparent waters, rolled along helplessly as if caught in a swirl. Only a few heads and arms are raised pathetically above the surface of the flood, catching all the light there is, and standing out against a sky where stripes of sombre blue, alternating with vertically arranged white dots, indicate the rain which pours down from the clouds, whilst the clarity above them seems to forecast the approaching end of the catastrophe.

There is hardly any scaling of the figures; they are too large in comparison with the ark, which itself is faulty in its perspective; in contrast to the figures and the ark, the waters are seen from a bird's-eye view. Yet a third dimension is most convincingly evoked by the varied and often daring foreshortening and occasional overlapping of the figures, and by the suggestion of atmosphere; and the entire composition has the rhythmical coherence of a 'dance macabre'.

Notwithstanding many traits which foretell the approach of medieval art the impact of a

ΛΑΕCΥΟΥΔΕΝΠΛΗΜCΟΥΔΙΑΤΟCΕΓΥΝΗΑΥΤΙΚΑΙ
ΕΙΠΩCΚΑΙΠΩCΠΟΙΗCΩΤΑΡΗΜΑΤΟΠΟΝΗΡΟΥ
ΤΟΥΠΟCΙΑΜΑΡΤΗCΟΜΑΙΕΝΑΝΤΙΟΝΤΟΥΘΥ
ΗΝΙΚΑΔΕΕΛΑΛΤΩΙΩCΗΦΗΜΕΡΑΝΕΞΗΜΕΡΑC
ΚΑΙΟΥΧΥΠΗΚΟΥCΕΝΑΥΤΗΚΑΘΕΥΔΕΙΝΜΕΤΑΗC
ΤΟΥCΥΝΓΕΝΕCΘΑΙΑΥΤΗ ΕΓΕΝΕΤΟ ΔΕΤΟΙΑΥΤΗ
ΤΗCΗΜΕΡΑCΕΙCΗΛΘΕΝΙΩCΗΦΕΙCΤΗΝΟΙΚΙΑΝ
ΛCΤΕΠΟΙΗCΑΙΤΑΕΡΓΑΛΥΤΟΥΚΑΙΟΥΘΕΙCΤΩΝΕΝΤΗ
ΟΙΚΙΑ ΕCΩΕΠΕCΠΑCΑΤΟΑΥΤΟΝΤΩΝΙΜΑΤΙΩΝ
ΛΕΓΟΥCΑΚΟΙΜΗΘΗΤΙΜΕΤΕΜΟΥΚΑΙΚΑΤΑΛΙΠΩΝ
ΤΑΙΜΑΤΙΑΑΥΤΟΥΕΝΤΑΙCΧΕΡCΕΙΝΑΥΤΗCΕΦΥΓΕΝΚ
ΕΞΗΛΘΕΝΕΞΩ ΚΑΙΕΓΕΝΕΤΟΩCΕΙΔΕΝΟΤΙ
ΚΥΠΟΜΑΤΙΑΕΝΤΑΙCΧΕΡCΙΝΑΥΤΟΥΕΝΤΑΙCΧΕΡCΙΝ
ΑΥΤΗCΚΑΙΕΦΥΓΕΝΚΑΙΕΞΗΛΘΕΝΕΞΩ

classical tradition on this painting is still very obvious. We are, indeed, reminded of Hellenistic wall-paintings. The co-existence of contrasting features in a single picture would find its
easiest explanation if we supposed that an early model had been imitated and transformed at a
later period.[4] The possibility of such a proceeding will be discussed below.

The pictures to Noah's Exit from the Ark and to the Establishment of the Covenant—the
other one-scene painting—are followed by that to the story of Noah's Drunkenness, which is
illustrated in Plate 2. This miniature is the last which is isolated from the text by framing lines.
But within this frame, figures and objects are painted directly against the purple of the page
which thus provides an abstract substitute for space. The ground has shrunk to a stripe so
narrow that it only just supplies the necessary room for the figures and accessories. The several
frieze-like scenes are presented according to the 'continuous'—or 'cyclic'—method of narration,
the same persons appearing and reappearing in various situations, standing on the same level
against the common background of the purple page. A highly stylized ornamental vine, which
is meant to symbolize Noah's husbandry, accompanies the figure groups. The first of them
consists of Noah with his three sons and his small grandson Canaan, whom he addresses with
a rhetorical gesture. Then we see the wicked son, Ham, beckoning to his brothers to witness
their father's shame; after this, the good sons walking backwards—a movement whose render-
ing exceeded the illustrator's capacity—and carrying the garment with which they are going to
cover Noah's nakedness; and then only Noah himself, sleeping in his house. Like the 'Flood',
this painting does not conform with the majority of the illustrations in so far as it shows a fusion,
and partly, even, a reversal in the order of the scenes. For the first group clearly illustrates the end
of the story, Noah's cursing of the child Canaan in consequence of his father Ham's treacherous
behaviour. In other representations of the subject, the first scene shows Noah pressing the grapes
or else testing them, in the company of his sons. This first scene has here been left out and replaced by the last, while the following stages of the story: Ham spying on his father, Ham
telling his brothers what he saw, the brothers' kindly action, have been condensed, Noah
appearing once only. These facts indicate that the Vienna Genesis must have been copied from
another manuscript which was even more explicit in its pictorial interpretation of the Bible
text.[5]

The figures are vivid and expressive in gesture and attitude, but being confined to the narrow
space of a shallow stage and moving in a plane parallel to the picture plane, they have neither
the fluidity nor the variety of posture which characterizes the figures appearing in the first picture, discussed above. The artist shows little inclination, or ability, to give the illusion of a third
dimension. It is characteristic that the foot of Noah's stool which is farthest away from the
beholder and would, therefore, be indicative of depth, is non-existent; the same is true of one of
the brother's legs in the middle group. Noah's house is derived from classical or near-classical
models, as can be seen from its similarity with Dido's house in the Vatican Virgil, a manuscript
dating from about A.D. 400 or later, but reflecting an older artistic inheritance.[6] The same
deep-set window which we find there seems here to be out of place. The coffered ceiling visible
in the Virgil painting has virtually disappeared in the present illustration; all that remains is an

ornamented band. And of two converging walls, only the one with the door has survived, being necessary for the understanding of the situation.

In spite of an essentially different artistic conception, both paintings, the 'Flood' and 'Noah's Drunkenness', have many details in common: the faces seen in profile are almost identical; certain colours—for example the pink of some garments—are exactly alike; the modelling of limbs with occasional high-lights and some sharp black contours is very similar in both pictures; in fact Noah, though his limbs are negligently drawn, is quite as 'classical' in his general appearance as any figure occurring in the 'Flood'. The reclining body looks alien in its surroundings and has definitely been inspired by some classical River God, taking us back in time for its original type as far as the well-known 'Nile' in the Vatican Museum.

When discussing our first illustration, we referred to ancient prototypes in order to explain its contrasting features. Here again we feel the presence of an ancient tradition; but in the present miniature, the alienation from classical conceptions has gone further than in the 'Flood', since it affects to a higher degree the spacial relationship of forms. If judged by itself, the 'Flood' is the greater masterpiece; but in spite—or rather because—of its shortcomings from the point of view of classical naturalism, our second example is better adapted to the page of the book, while the first, being spatially self-contained, tends to lose its decorative unity.

All the following pages up to Abraham's meeting with Melchisedek have been lost, nor has the story of Abraham's later years been fully preserved. However, his servant's wooing of Rebekah is illustrated by three paintings containing several scenes which follow each other in two superposed rows. Plate 3, the middle one, shows a specific variation of the two-row system. A walled-in town, small in size and painted according to a well-known post-classical tradition, as if seen from above, as well as the road lined with milestones which emerges from it, stand on the upper row seen against the purple of the page. But on the left, the part of the road on which Rebekah descends slopes down to the banks of the spring which, being placed at an angle, forms a connecting link between the upper and the lower row. The group of Rebekah, giving the servant a drink, and also the first of the camels, are seen against the hillside which is painted in a brownish tone; the other camels, however, appear frieze-like against the purple ground. On the left, then, the action takes place within the defined space of a fairly consistent landscape; but on the right we are faced with an abstract arrangement in two rows; and we find the same symptoms of a negation of space as in our former illustration; the bodies and legs of the camels are only shown as far as they can be spread out into the foreground, and the heads which are needed to indicate the number of the herd are irrationally squeezed in between the town and the road which belong to the upper row. The painting is an accurate and vivid illustration of the story, though it contains one figure which does not occur in any biblical text: resting on the bank is the nymph of the spring, one of those personifications which we know so well from classical and post-classical works of all kinds, as well as from later Byzantine manuscripts (e.g. the Joshua rotulus, see n. 15), and which, notwithstanding some changes in their attributes, can be traced back to ancient mythological figures in classical wall-paintings.

Plate 4, which originally was separated from our last illustration by several pages, belongs to the majority of the Genesis pictures, in that the two rows, in which the story unrolls itself in an uninterrupted flow, remain quite independent of each other. The stripe which stands for the ground is throughout very narrow, whereby certain omissions become necessary—only the upper part of Esau is visible, as he sits at the table to eat the fatal pottage. The only other accessory is Jacob's cooking stove which, like the table, is a necessary 'stage property', of essential importance for the understanding of the plot. The figures are on the whole similar to those of the other illustrations, though, perhaps owing to the narrow interspace, those in the lower row are stockier than usual. Their movements and gestures are expressive rather than anatomically correct: Esau, addressing himself to Jacob, is rather hovering over, than standing on, the ground, though his gesture suggests most convincingly his eagerness to get food, as well as the solemnity of his oath; also, his hurrying forward movement when returning from the hunt is not completely equilibrated. One figure only forms an exception: the youth who follows Esau and who, like the nymph in the former illustration, is not mentioned in any text, proceeds in the same hurried fashion. But the turning of his head provides the necessary counterpoise, which becomes even more accentuated by the burden he carries; and together with the hounds he forms a group which is balanced in its composition. Again we feel that this group may well have been inspired by some remote classical model.

In the manuscript, this painting is followed by one which illustrates Jacob's and Rebekah's stay with the Philistines. Then, after what must be regarded as a long gap of at least 16 pages, we find four paintings which describe in a bucolic manner some of the events of Jacob's life with Laban. The first of them, Plate 5 shows, as does Plate 3, a variation, but of a different kind, of the double row system. For here most of the picture surface has been converted into a 'terrace landscape', descending from a type created in late Antiquity; this landscape is formed by broken rocks which, with their upper surfaces illuminated by patchy high-lights, are seen from a bird's-eye view against a green background spread out like a vertically displayed carpet. Yet the frieze composition remains recognizable in the upper part of the painting and is very obvious in the lower. In the first, we find Jacob and Laban discussing the division of the herds; together with some formalized flowers and a conventional 'mushroom' tree, they are placed approximately on the same level, just below the line which is meant to represent the horizon and where the purple of the page takes over and stands for the sky. The second part is more complex: on the left we see Jacob in the action of separating the herd; a young shepherd pulls one of the animals towards the middle, where Laban is seated on a rocky slope, directing the proceedings; on the right, another young servant, who is obviously driving away his flock, stops and looks back, perhaps waiting for stragglers. As in the former illustration, the figures in the lower row, which serves as foreground, are smaller than those standing against the sky-line; here, however, within a coherent landscape setting the difference in size of the figures gives the impression of an 'inverted perspective'. It is a natural consequence of the two row system, that the spatial relation between the figures and the landscape background is altogether a loose one. It is mainly indicated by the slope with the seated Laban and by the zigzagging herd, which alone are independent of the front line to which the majority of figures and animals are confined. Jacob's story is continued in eight illustrations, most of them in two rows, but several chapters of the story are altogether missing from the manuscript.

The greatest prominence, however, was given to the Joseph legend, to which twenty-one of the existing paintings are devoted, and which originally must have occupied at least double that number. This is not exceptional in Early Christian art. The predilection for this legend is indeed characteristic of Jewish and Early Christian literature and finds its reflection in the art of the period on many of the surviving sarcophagi, on ivories and on other works.

Plate 6 (fol. XVI, 31) shows on the whole the same characteristic abstract arrangement which we know from Plate 4, and which occurs in so many other of the paintings. Yet the single scenes extend farther into space. The classical colonnade, though inaccurate in its perspective and out of proportion with the figures, forms a convincing semicircle around the couch of Potiphar's wife; and the isolated door through which Joseph is going to escape, though faulty in design, and a mere 'stage property' which leads into nothingness, suggests by its diagonal position a third dimension, and is reminiscent of the doors which we know from illustrated copies of classical plays.[7] The whole scene, in the rhythmical fluidity and energy of its composition, has a most satisfactory coherence: each figure, as it were, stands within its own frame, the swinging door taking up Joseph's movement and accentuating the impetus of his flight.

With this scene the text has come to an end, but the picture continues. Beyond the door, Joseph looks back towards the incident of his temptation, thus providing a link between this and the following scenes. For he finds himself among the women of Potiphar's household, whose occupations are rendered in a succession of attractive and lively little genre pictures. The single groups are well balanced and, as a consequence of the occasional overlapping of figures, and of the curves of their movement, they convey some feeling of depth, in spite of being confined to the narrow standing line. This painting, with its subtle colouring, is one of the most delightful in the whole book. (See p. 7 for a reproduction of the full page.)

So far our illustrations have been taken from the first part of the manuscript, the part in which the first scribe was responsible for the writing. The two following examples belong to the second series of paintings which, in their greater economy, correspond to a less condensed text. Plate 7 shows Joseph and his fellow-prisoners within the walls of a building which is probably meant to be circular and from which the vault has been removed. The chief butler is rejoicing at Joseph's interpretation of his dream whilst the chief baker is woefully listening to the prophecy regarding his own. The figures on the right are supposed to be the friendly keeper of the dungeon, talking to his wife, a personage not occurring in the text. He sits in front of a classical column crowned by a sun-dial, a feature known from Pompeian paintings. A square building and some trees or bushes are partly hidden by the prison walls. The introduction of these features is suggestive of depth, though the figures themselves are again spread out in the foreground, moving parallel to the plane of the picture. Objects and figures are painted directly against the uniform ground of the parchment. But here the ground has lost some of its neutrality and evokes atmosphere. For in this painting we feel a tendency towards a colouristic rather than a linear interpretation. Sometimes the clearness of forms seems to dissolve in the surrounding air, the painter giving the illusion of their appearance rather than their objective definition. This applies particularly to his treatment of foliage.

In fact, the purple ground has completely disappeared from the majority of the later pictures, and they have their background well defined by paint. Plate 8 may serve as a typical example; it comprises several scenes: on the left, one of Joseph's brothers finds in his ass's saddlebag the money which had been paid out in Egypt, a fact which he then puts excitedly before the others; and on the right, the brothers tell Jacob 'all that befell them'. The continuous method still prevails; but the element of movement, so obvious in the frieze compositions, has come to a standstill. Everything seems to happen simultaneously within a landscape whose depth is suggested by the sizing of the figures, who are not confined to the foreground plane, as well as by the hazy shading, which softens the contours of hills and buildings appearing in the distance.

In these various ways of opening a perspective into a third dimension, the painter shows himself still bound to the classical tradition. Other features, however, which appear in this picture are decidedly non-classical. The preponderance of the heads against the other parts of the bodies is even more marked here than in our former examples, feet and hands being drawn with extreme negligence; and, again, wherever several figures are assembled in a group, the more distant ones are only partially presented: some feet are altogether missing, some heads are sketched in rough contours only.

In fact, most of the paintings of the second series do not compare favourably in quality with those of the first. Though they too are generally lively in style, and though they have a certain colouristic charm, the very lightness of touch tends to degenerate into carelessness.

Notwithstanding all the many differences which exist between the first and the second set of illustrations, they also show overriding similarities. The types of the figures, the garments they wear, occasional dark linear contours alternating with a subtle modelling in light and shade—all these traits appear in pictures which are scattered all over the manuscript; and over and over again we are faced with an attitude wavering between a two-dimensional and a three-dimensional conception of things.

*　　*　　*　　*

The Vienna Genesis had already been assigned an important place in all books on Early Christian art,[8] long before the issue of the complete photographic publication of its illustrations in 1895. The introduction to this publication by Wickhoff, the doyen of the Vienna school of art history, in which he set out his ideas on the development of Roman art, has become a standard work.[9] By applying the method of detailed stylistic criticism to the study of the miniatures, he came to the conclusion that the separate, still unbound sections of the manuscript were distributed among different craftsmen in one workshop. He believed that four men, the 'miniaturist' and the 'colourist', each with an assistant, were responsible for the illustrations of the first part, and three others, whom he calls the 'illusionists', for the second; and he suggests that the latter had been trained in the tradition of late-classical wall and panel painting, whilst the former, in their perfect handling of the continuous method of narration, represented a new trend in book illustration, which was to survive all through the Middle Ages. According to Wickhoff, the combination of an illusionistic style and of the continuous method was a typically Roman achievement. The Vienna Genesis, as he saw it, was a manifestation of late-classical art in a transition stage; he therefore believed that its date could not be later than the IV Century A.D. Some of Wickhoff's views have been accepted and still are regarded as valid. His attribution of the illustrations to several painters has found general recognition, though some later scholars differ with him, but also with one another, as to the exact number of collaborators and the precise scope of their work; and nobody doubts the correctness of his statement as to the stylistic ambiguity of the pictures. In other respects, however, his theories proved to be untenable.

It is now generally believed that the Vienna Genesis originated in one of the Eastern provinces in the Byzantine Empire. A number of sound reasons speak in favour of this assumption. For one, it has to be remembered that the manuscript is written in Greek; and, though purple vellum became a highly valued medium in the West, it was first produced in the East. We are told that the craft of using purple dyes on parchment was practised by Syrian monks as early as the IV Century.

Another argument runs as follows: the Vienna Genesis contains a few marginal lines written in a medieval Italian dialect, which might be taken as a confirmation of Wickhoff's thesis, that the codex was actually written in Italy. But there is another detail about the manuscript which must be taken into consideration: when it was transferred to the Imperial Library it was bound up with two folios of another ancient purple codex. This was a fragment of a non-illustrated Greek Gospel book, other parts of which were discovered in various libraries; the most important of those fragments had been found in Caesarea in Cappadocia; a second fragment, according to an old tradition, was presented to Pope Innocent VIII by the King of Cyprus.

All these facts, taken together, give much credibility to the assumption that the Vienna Genesis, together with the Gospel fragment, was brought to Italy from the East at the time of the Crusades, before it found its way to Austria.

An important phase in the attempts to find out the date and the origin of the Vienna Genesis was reached when it appeared that two other manuscripts survived, which had their roots in the same artistic milieu; for from then onwards the investigations into the history of our codex could proceed from a wider basis.

Wickhoff himself, when describing examples of the continuous style other than the Genesis, mentions the 'Codex Rossanensis', so called since it is kept in the Cathedral of Rossano in Calabria; but he failed to notice how much this manuscript had in common with the Genesis.[10] The other affiliated work is the 'Codex Sinopensis' in Paris, which was purchased in Sinope. Both are New Testament fragments and are intimately connected with each other. This close relationship seems remarkable if we consider the extreme paucity of pre-iconoclastic illustrated manuscripts which have come down to us; in fact, the Rossanensis and the Sinopensis are the only illustrated Greek Gospel books of this period which survive—just as the Cotton Bible and the Vienna Genesis are the only illustrated Greek Old Testament fragments which we possess.

The Gospel books have to convey a message of the utmost importance. In the Rossanensis, on the bottom part of each page, four prophets holding script tablets with Old Testament quotations point dramatically upwards to an illustration of a Gospel story which is vibrant with emotion. In the Sinopensis, two Old Testament figures, impressive by their very size, stand each on one side of the Gospel illustrations, holding a script tablet with one hand, while the other is stretched out against the picture between them.

Undoubtedly, the feeling of pathos, of poignant tension, inherent in these pages is absent from the Vienna Genesis pictures, most of which are conceived in a simple and direct narrative style, which is characterized by a bucolic element and by lively novelistic features. Yet we find a number of striking analogies among all three manuscripts. They are all written in the same Greek script, its metal shining against the purple vellum of the page; and it is possible to point out in the Genesis illustrations a number of features, which can be paralleled in the other two codices: we find certain figures in all three manuscripts which are as similar in type as they are in the expressiveness of their faces and in their characteristic gestures, and they wear the same costumes; some animals, some buildings and other objects appearing in the different codices have great resemblance to one another.

The analogies between the Genesis on the one hand and the Gospel books on the other provide ample proof for the assumption of an Eastern origin of our manuscript, for the investigations into the iconography of the Gospel fragment have shed new light on the problem involved. As far back as 1920 A. Baumstarck suggested that the illustrations of the Codex Rossanensis corresponded with the pericopes from the Gospel which were read during Lent within the orbit of the Patriarchate of Antioch in the second half of the VI Century.[11] And A. Grabar, in his recent facsimile publication of the Sinopensis,[12] emphasizes the fact that the juxtaposition of Gospel scenes with Biblical figures as antitypical—i.e. Old Testament—witnesses, was a feature which originated in the Syro-Palestinensian sphere; similar witnesses, different in their aspect, but identical as to their function, appear also on VI-Century ivories usually attributed to that region, such as the famous ivory throne of Maximian in Ravenna, or the St Lupicin diptych in Paris.

The type of Christ himself, as he appears in both Gospel fragments, with severe features and long hair and beard, is generally attributed to the Syro-Palestinensian tradition which extended over Asia Minor and the adjoining part of Mesopotamia. Some architectural types point towards Syria proper.

Wherever the manuscripts originated, one thing is certain: notwithstanding the strong Oriental flavour of their paintings, they were influenced by the art of Byzantium. Many of the non-classical features of the Vienna Genesis are typically Byzantine. Such characteristics are: the tendency to bring the figures as far as possible into the foreground and only partly to represent those which could only be accommodated in a second plane; the way in which some of the figures hover insecurely over the ground and in which others hurry on in an exaggerated forward motion; the negligent drawing of hands and feet.

Some items point more particularly to the Justinian era (527–565). It is illuminating in this regard to study, as Gerstinger has done, the various costumes and head-dresses. The purple chlamys with the tablion as well as the diadems worn by persons of high standing are those we know from the Imperial portraits of the Justinian period—Pharaoh's diadem, in fact, is identical with that worn by Theodora on the mosaic in San Vitale in Ravenna. Pharaoh's body-guard and his courtiers are dressed in uniforms which also can be paralleled in Justinian works; the 'segments', the ornamented pieces of material which appear as dark patches on Joseph's garment, occur in works of that time in exactly the same fashion; the coiffure of Potiphar's wife is that of Byzantine empresses of the VI Century. A number of other parallels could be added.

P. Buberl, who meticulously studied the Vienna Genesis by means of greatly enlarged photographs and who wrote two important articles intended as complementary to Gerstinger's *magnum opus*,[13] makes an additional observation. According to him, the paintings may be copies made at a slightly later date from a model of the Justinian period; he states that he finds a carelessness of execution in the pictures which is not compatible with the relatively high standard of their composition; and he thinks that the collaboration of several hands on one manuscript points towards the activity of a prolific scriptorium engaged in mass production rather than in the creation of original works, and which scriptorium may well have been situated in one of the big monasteries either in the town or in the surroundings of Antioch.

In agreement with other contemporary scholars Buberl, as well as Gerstinger, is far from suggesting that a work of the Justinian period could ever be regarded as the ultimate prototype of the Vienna Genesis. Even our short description of only a limited number of illustrations has shown remarkable divergencies of style which exist, not only between the various paintings, but sometimes even within one single picture, late-classical features being fused with others which attest a subsequent development. Also, certain traits in the iconography of the miniatures (Plate 2 e.g.) are not exactly paralleled in the text and find their explanation only if they are compared with other illustrations of the same subject.

This complex character of the Vienna Genesis is by no means an isolated phenomenon; it has analogies in other ancient manuscripts. It is only natural that once a text has been provided with pictures its future illustrators will be influenced by the first illustrations. In other words, this first illustrated manuscript will serve as an archetype for later illustrations of the same text. But we would grossly simplify the facts if we imagined that the copying and re-copying of the original illustrations proceeded, as it were, in one unbroken sequence. It is only plausible to believe that, perhaps soon after its creation, a number of copies were made independently from the archetype and that some of these copies again gave rise to a number of new, illustrated manuscripts; also that, in the course of time, the original pictures underwent perceptible changes which varied in different copies—we are thus reminded of a complicated family tree with many diverging and interlacing branches. The story might be even more in-volved than this: one or more illustrated versions of a particularly important text might have been produced independently from one another in various artistic centres, so that we would have to assume the coexistence of several archetypes. Also, illustrations of an earlier text of a re-lated character, either in manuscripts or else in some other medium, could have some influence on the formation of the one or the other picture of an otherwise different, mainly original, set of illustrations.

These many possibilities have to be taken into consideration and to be confronted with actual facts in any attempt to delineate the history of early Bible illustration in general and, in parti-cular, to reconstitute the archetype of the Vienna Genesis.

The two scholars mentioned above, who have devoted the most extensive studies to the Vienna Genesis, Gerstinger and Buberl, in the course of their research, reached different views of the problems involved. Gerstinger thinks it most likely that the first narrative cycles of Bible illus-trations—as opposed to the symbolic representations we know from early Catacomb paintings and sarcophagi—were formed in the IV, or even already in the III Century, and that they first appeared in manuscripts. Though fully aware of the fact that any endeavour to reconstruct the archetype of the Genesis is bound to be tentative since we do not know what intermediary links between that remote manuscript and the actual codex have been lost, he suggests that the idyllic, bucolic character of our manuscript is best explained if we assume that its model originated in the IV Century, against the background of IV-Century literature (Gregory of Nyssa, Minucius Felix, Prudentius etc.); and he believes that Alexandria was the most likely place where the immense task of inventing pictures for the Bible stories might have been un-dertaken, thus providing a basis for so vast a section of future artistic activities; he finds that all the early cycles of Bible illustration are essentially connected with each other and must there-fore have a common origin. He does not exclude the possibility of there having been influ-ences at work which came from certain Gnostic and other sectarian and heretical circles, also from Hellenized Jewry.

The type of manuscript which Gerstinger visualizes as the archetype of the Vienna Genesis, as Wickhoff and others had done before him, is a roll with continuous pictures. As we know, the parchment codex was preceded by the papyrus roll. And it was assumed by a number of scholars that the illustrated rolls primarily consisted of an uninterrupted sequence of pictures with a short text or eventually without text of any kind. This theory was mainly based on two documents: Trajan's column, whose reliefs, winding spiral-like around it in a continuous frieze, were considered to be copies of a picture roll;[14] and on an actual picture roll, the Joshua roll in the Vatican Library (Pal. Graec. 431), which contains a picture frieze running con-tinuously over jointed sheets of parchment, and which was for a time considered as the most ancient of all surviving illustrated manuscripts, though Gerstinger and others with him regard it as a X Century copy of an early original.[15]

Such a roll, then, would have been the model which was copied by the illustrators, at least with very few exceptions (our Plate 1)—of the first part of the Vienna Genesis (our Plates

2–6). These men—or perhaps illustrators working at some intermediate stage—would have divided the roll pictures of their model to suit the format of the codex, frequently putting, for economy's sake, one row above the other, and uniting in various instances both rows into one compositional unit. The illustrators of the second part (our Plates 7 and 8) had presumably worked from a different model, containing pictures with painted backgrounds, and with figures spatially related to their surroundings. Such pictures were already in keeping with the format of the codex and, in fact, some of the earliest illustrated manuscripts which have come down to us, the Itala fragments attributed to the end of the IV Century, the slightly later Virgil in the Vatican Library[16] and the Iliad in the Ambrosiana contain paintings of that very kind.[17]

Since he regards the landscape backgrounds in the row compositions of the Vienna Genesis as later additions, Gerstinger must believe that their archetype was conceived in a rather simple linear style; but otherwise he refrains from describing in a more precise way his mental image of the early lost manuscript.

The American scholar Charles R. Morey is more definite in trying to delineate his own ideas of this archetype.[18] He agrees with Gerstinger in thinking that it originated in Alexandria, and that it was a roll which at a given time was divided into single pictures; but he assumes that it had three-dimensional painted background landscapes of a Hellenistic character with figures well placed in space, and that it was these same landscapes which, after having undergone a transformation into two dimensions, still survived in the background paintings of our actual manuscript.

P. Buberl's views differ in many ways from both Gerstinger's and Morey's. He thinks that the plan of illustrating any single book of the Bible—for it is obvious from the vast number of illustrated scenes in the earliest documents that each book was regarded and treated as a complete entity—could have taken place only after the Christian victory in the IV Century, at a time when the papyrus roll had already been replaced by the parchment codex. He refutes altogether the roll theory, particularly in the form which had been accepted by Morey. For he considers papyrus an unsuitable medium for the use of rich and differentiated colours which anyway would tend to flake off with the frequent rolling and unrolling of the rotulus.

He admits that the archetype of the Cotton Bible was created at Alexandria, an assumption justified by iconographic data—Joseph's granaries, for example, have the appearance of pyramids. But he believes that another type of early Genesis illustration, the one which survives in the Vienna codex, had its origin in Antioch. The famous theological school of Antioch was particularly concerned with Genesis studies, a fact which would account for the emergence of an independent cycle of illustration, perhaps in the time of John Chrysostomos (345–407). A theologian would have instructed and supervised the artist, or the group of artists, who invented the illustrations to the Biblical text; this would not exclude the possibility that some of the illustrations were inspired by existing wall paintings or by minor works in another medium.

The Justinian manuscript was presumably removed from the archetype by a number of intermediate copies; and it is quite possible that the different groups of later illustrators had different copies in hand, and that the 'illusionists' were working from a model which faith-fully reproduced the archetype, while the artists of the first part were working from a later copy in which—always a small number of pictures excepted—the earlier style had been re-interpreted.

K. Weitzmann, in his much-discussed book *Illustrations in Roll and Codex*,[19] reverts to the roll theory, but on a completely different basis. Founding his studies on the surviving frag-ments of Greek illustrated papyrus rolls, which extend in time from the early II Century B.C. to the V Century A.D., he comes to the following conclusions: in the 'papyrus style' where the texts were written in columns, the illustrations were usually placed within the writing columns, either immediately above or below the particular passage to which they belong. Some of these illustrations were mere diagrams which served to explain scientific texts. Others—illustrations to Homer among them—contained a wealth of figural scenes. But these too were of a simple, linear kind; none of them were framed, and they appeared directly against the neutral ground of the papyrus. The parchment codex came into being at about A.D. 100, and roll and codex existed side by side until some time between the IV and V Centuries when the roll was generally abandoned for the codex. When columns of writing, with pictures incorporated in the text, had to be transferred from roll to codex, this could be done without submitting them to any immediate alterations. In the process of assimilation to the new format, however, the number of columns of writing was gradually reduced to one; and, in a parallel process, the former column-pictures, each of which consisted of a single scene or 'iconographic unit', were put together into one row which at first was placed irregularly in the text. Then followed the superposition of rows and, finally, the miniatures came to occupy the entire page; they were surrounded by frames, and their area was filled in with a painted background. In fact, the Itala Bible, the Vatican Virgil and the Ambrosian Iliad were already decorated with full-page pictures. The type of decoration, preserved in the Vienna Genesis, represents, according to Weitzmann, an important step in this evolution, since the illustrators, in reserving the lower half of each page for the paintings and the upper for the writing, arrived 'artistically speaking at a more systematic and unified distribution of the pictures than had been known hitherto'.

In analysing the illustrations, Weitzmann finds that the row pictures of the first part can be divided into single units of approximately equal width, and he thinks it obvious that originally they were column pictures. Some of them, being painted directly against the parchment ground, had remained true to the papyrus style; to others, landscape backgrounds had been added. In the second part, the addition of landscape backgrounds created spatial unity to the scenes and gave the necessary width to single scenes which, without them, would have been too narrow for the picture area.

Weitzmann does not, in the book under discussion, go into any of the questions concerning the origin of the earliest Biblical illustrations; as we shall see, he has treated this subject in great detail in another study.

These various views can be summarized as follows: the Vienna Genesis goes back to a late-classical archetype which was formed in the IV Century A.D. in one of the great centres of Eastern Hellenism, either in Alexandria or else in Antioch. It may still have had the format of a roll, or already that of a codex. We do not know the kind and number of copies which intervened between this archetype and the Vienna Genesis. We must, however, consider the possibility that the illustrators who painted its first series of pictures followed a different model from those who worked on the second.

One thing is certain: each theory taken separately, and all taken together, fully explain the differences of style which appear in our manuscript; for they show that this style evolved from diverse layers of artistic development, separated from each other by centuries.

Recent discoveries have helped to widen, in an unexpected way, the basis for the studies of early Bible illustrations. By far the most important is that of the Synagogue of Dura-Europos on the Euphrates, made by the Yale University Expedition at the beginning of the thirties.[20] The walls of this Synagogue are covered with frescoes illustrating episodes from the Pentateuch, many of which are of a narrative character and are arranged in superposed rows. The frescoes belong to the middle of the III Century A.D.; but the wide range and diversity of their subjects, as well as the fact that their provincial Mesopotamian style contains many elements of Hellenistic lineage, indicate that the painters were rooted in an existing tradition. This tradition must have originated in one of the artistic centres of Eastern Hellenism and may well go back to pre-Christian times; and most probably it found its first expression in the illustration of manuscripts. Weitzmann, indeed, suggests that soon after it had been translated from Hebrew into Greek (III Century B.C.), the Septuagint was illustrated in the Hellenized Jewish milieu of Alexandria, and that some of these early illustrated manuscripts may have served as intermediaries between classical papyrus rolls and Christian book illustration.[21] Besides the canonical version, other legendary versions of the Bible stories must have been illustrated at an early period. For a number of the scenes in the Dura Synagogue cannot be regarded as illustrations of the Septuagint proper, but are based on Jewish legends.[22] Reflections of such legends are still visible in some features which appear in Early Christian and Byzantine works.[23] They also occur in our Genesis. Fol. XV, 30, illustrates Joseph's departure from his father's house, and his meeting with the man who directs him towards Dothan where he finds his brothers. But in the miniature he is, previous to this encounter, guided by an angel who is not mentioned in the text. According to a legend, however, it is the angel Gabriel who shows him the way.[24] Is it possible that other supplementary figures—the youth who follows Esau from the hunt, the women of Potiphar's household and a few others—are not novellistic features but also belong to some not yet explored text? It is interesting, in this connection, to mention the discovery of a XVI-Century manuscript containing non-canonical Joseph stories which faithfully reproduce the style of an Early Christian original, and this style is most intimately connected with that of the Vienna Genesis.[25]

It is a frequent experience for archaeologists working on an ancient site to find unexpectedly, in the course of their digging, an even older site underneath. And it happens that, by uncovering one layer after the other, they reach into hitherto unsuspected strata of historical evidence.

Time seems to be receding before their very eyes.

The students of ancient manuscript illustrations are less fortunate, in so far as they hardly ever meet with tangible, irrefutable proofs. Their work, however, is equally exciting. By studying the manuscripts in a critical spirit, by comparing them with each other and with works of art of all sorts, by making use of literary and historical documents and by interpreting archaeological discoveries, they too have succeeded in gradually going further and further back into the past and can evoke in their own minds and in that of their readers the images of things which have once existed but presumably will never be recovered.

Here the Vienna Genesis is of special importance. For its study leads us back to events which have been of the greatest consequence for the future evolution of art, calling up the epoch when the tales contained in the Book of Books were for the first time translated into visual form.

NOTE ON THE CAPTIONS

The captions to the illustrations show the corresponding passages of the Septuagint according to the Authorized Version. The brackets indicate the main omissions which have taken place in the manuscript. For textual and palaeographic details cf. W. v. Hartel and F. Wickhoff, op. cit., pp. 102–141 (see note 9) and Gerstinger, op. cit., pp. 36–40 (see note 2).

Against Wickhoff's seven masters, Morey believes that six, Gerstinger and Buberl that eight, masters collaborated on the manuscript. The views of these four scholars are indicated in the captions.

The monochrome illustration on p. 7 reproduces a full page of the manuscript.

The reproductions are made by courtesy of the Vienna National Library.

PLATE 1

Fol. II, 3. Genesis VII, 19–VIII, 13.

Wickhoff: first master (Miniaturist)
Morey: first master
Gerstinger: first master
Buberl: first master

VII, 19 And the waters prevailed exceedingly upon the earth; and all the high hills, that
were under the whole heaven, were covered.

20 Fifteen cubits upward did the waters prevail; and the mountains were covered.

21 And all flesh died that moved upon the earth, both of fowl, and of cattle, and of
beast, and of every creeping thing that creepeth upon the earth, and every man:

22 All in whose nostrils was the breath of life, of all that was in the dry land, died.

23 [And every living substance was destroyed which was upon the face of the ground,
both man, and cattle, and the creeping things, and the fowl of the heaven; and they
were destroyed from the earth:] and Noah only remained alive, and they that were
with him in the ark.

24 And the waters prevailed upon the earth an hundred and fifty days.

VIII, 1 [And God remembered Noah, and every living thing, and all the cattle that was
with him in the ark:] and God made a wind to pass over the earth, and the waters
asswaged;

2 The fountains also of the deep and the windows of heaven were stopped, and the
rain from heaven was restrained;

3 And the waters returned from off the earth continually: and after the end of the
hundred and fifty days the waters were abated.

4 And the ark rested in the seventh month, on the seventeenth day of the month, upon
the mountains of Ararat.

[5 And the waters decreased continually until the tenth month: in the tenth month,
on the first day of the month, were the tops of the mountains seen.

6 And it came to pass at the end of forty days, that Noah opened the window of the
ark which he had made:

7 And he sent forth a raven, which went forth to and fro, until the waters were dried
up from off the earth.

[Continued on page 24

22

8 Also he sent forth a dove from him, to see if the waters were abated from off the face of the ground;

9 But the dove found no rest for the sole of her foot, and she returned unto him into the ark, for the waters were on the face of the whole earth: then he put forth his hand, and took her, and pulled her in unto him into the ark.

10 And he stayed yet other seven days; and again he sent forth the dove out of the ark;

11 And the dove came in to him in the evening; and, lo, in her mouth was an olive leaf pluckt off: so Noah knew that the waters were abated from off the earth.

12 And he stayed yet other seven days; and sent forth the dove; which returned not again unto him any more.]

13 And it came to pass in the six hundredth and first year, in the first month, the first day of the month, the waters were dried up from off the earth: and Noah removed the covering of the ark, and looked, and, behold, the face of the ground was dry.

PLATE 2

Fol. III, 6. Genesis IX, 20–27.

Wickhoff:	first master
Morey:	first master
Gerstinger:	first master
Buberl:	first master

IX, 20 And Noah began to be an husbandman, and he planted a vineyard:

21 And he drank of the wine, and was drunken; and he was uncovered within his tent.

22 And Ham, the father of Canaan, saw the nakedness of his father, and told his two brethren without.

23 And Shem and Japheth took a garment, and laid it upon both their shoulders, and went backward, [and covered the nakedness of their father; and their faces were backward,] and they saw not their father's nakedness.

24 And Noah awoke from his wine, and knew what his younger son had done unto him.

25 And he said, Cursed be Canaan; a servant of servants shall he be unto his brethren.

26 And he said, Blessed be the Lord God of Shem; and Canaan shall be his servant.

27 God shall enlarge Japheth, and he shall dwell in the tents of Shem; and Canaan shall be his servant.

PLATE 4

Fol. VIII, 15. Genesis XXV, 27–34.

Wickhoff:	first master
Morey:	first master
Gerstinger:	second master
Buberl:	second master

XXV, 27 And the boys grew: and Esau was a cunning hunter, a man of the field; and Jacob was a plain man, dwelling in tents.

28 And Isaac loved Esau, because he did eat of his venison: but Rebekah loved Jacob.

29 And Jacob sod pottage: and Esau came from the field, and he was faint.

30 And Esau said to Jacob, Feed me, I pray thee, with that same red pottage; for I am faint: [therefore was his name called Edom.]

31 And Jacob said, Sell me this day thy birthright.

32 And Esau said, Behold, I am at the point to die: and what profit shall this birthright do to me?

33 And Jacob said, Swear to me this day; and he sware unto him: and he sold his birthright unto Jacob.

34 Then Jacob gave Esau bread and pottage of lentiles; and he [did eat and drink, and] rose up, and went his way: thus Esau despised his birthright.

PLATE 5

Fol. IX, 17. Genesis XXX, 30–34.

Wickhoff:	first master
Morey:	second master
Gerstinger:	third master
Buberl:	third master

XXX, 30 [For it was little which thou hadst before I came, and it is now increased unto a multitude;] and the Lord hath blessed thee since my coming: and now when shall I provide for mine own house also?

31 And he said, What shall I give thee? And Jacob said, Thou shalt not give me any thing: if thou wilt do this thing for me, I will again feed and keep thy flock.

32 I will pass through all thy flock to day, removing from thence all the speckled and spotted cattle, and all the brown cattle among the sheep, and the spotted and speckled among the goats: and of such shall be my hire.

33 So shall my righteousness answer for me in time to come, when it shall come for my hire before thy face: every one that is not speckled and spotted among the goats, and brown among the sheep, that shall be counted stolen with me.

34 And Laban said, Behold, I would it might be according to thy word.

PLATE 6

Fol. XVI, 31. Genesis XXXIX, 9–13.

Wickhoff: third master (Colorist)
Morey: third master
Gerstinger: fifth master
Buberl: fifth master

XXXIX, 9 There is none greater in this house than I; neither hath he kept back any thing from me but thee, because thou art his wife: how then can I do this great wickedness, and sin against God?

10 And it came to pass, as she spake to Joseph day by day, that he hearkened not unto her, to lie by her, or to be with her.

11 And it came to pass about this time, that Joseph went into the house to do his business; and there was none of the men of the house there within.

12 And she caught him by his garment, saying, Lie with me: and he left his garment in her hand, and fled, and got him out.

13 And it came to pass, when she saw that he had left his garment in her hand, and was fled forth, . . .

A full-page monochrome reproduction of this page is included on page 7.

PLATE 7

Fol. XVII, 33. Genesis XL, 14–19

Wickhoff:	fifth master (1. Illusionist)
Morey:	fourth master
Gerstinger:	sixth master
Buberl:	sixth master

XL, 14 [But think on me when it shall be well with thee, and shew kindness, I pray thee, unto me, and make mention of me unto Pharaoh, and bring me] out of this house:

15 For indeed I was stolen away out of the land of the Hebrews: and here also have I done nothing that they should put me into the dungeon.

16 When the chief baker saw that the interpretation was good, he said unto Joseph, I also was in my dream, and, behold, I had three white baskets on my head:

17 And in the uppermost basket there was of all manner of bakemeats for Pharaoh; and the birds did eat them out of the basket upon my head.

18 And Joseph answered and said, This is the interpretation thereof: The three baskets are three days:

19 Yet within three days shall Pharaoh lift up thy head from off thee, and shall hang thee on a tree; and the birds shall eat thy flesh from off thee.

PLATE 8

Fol. XIX, 38. Genesis XLII, 26–31.

Wickhoff: sixth master (2. Illusionist)
Morey: fifth master
Gerstinger: seventh master
Buberl: eighth master

XLII, 26 And they laded their asses with the corn, and departed thence.

27 And as one of them opened his sack to give his ass provender in the inn, he espied his money; for, behold, it was in his sack's mouth.

28 And he said unto his brethren, My money is restored; and, lo, it is even in my sack: and their heart failed them, and they were afraid, saying one to another, What is this that God hath done unto us?

29 And they came unto Jacob their father unto the land of Canaan, and told him all that befell unto them; saying,

30 The man, who is the lord of the land, spake roughly to us, and took us for spies of the country.

31 And we said unto him, We are true men; we are no spies:

NOTES

[1] This manuscript was badly damaged by fire, but it has been possible to reconstruct its illustrations with the aid of later surviving works based on the same prototype; the most important are: a mosaic cycle in St Marco in Venice and the Genesis pictures in some Carolingian Bibles. Cf. J. J. Tikkanen, Die Genesismosaiken v. St Marco in Venedig u. ihr Verhältnis z. d. Min. d. Cottonbibel, Helsingfors, 1889. W. Köhler, Die Schule von Tours, I, Berlin, 1933. The miniatures of the Cotton Bible differ from those of the Vienna Genesis in iconography and in style. They are framed, rather static, the almost frontal figures arranged in a line.

[2] H. Gerstinger, Die Wiener Genesis, Vienna, 1931.

[3] In the St Marco cycle the three stages of the story are represented in three separate illustrations.

[4] R. Bianchi Bandinelli, La composizione del diluvio nella Genesi di Vienna, *Mitteilungen d. Deutschen Archäolog. Instit., Röm. Abt., 62, 1955,* suggests that the classical, monumental character of this particular illustration is due to a model which was a III-Century wall painting.

[5] This story as well is more fully illustrated in the St Marco cycle.

[6] Cf. notes 16, 17.

[7] A few Carolingian copies of Terence faithfully reproduce classical prototypes.

[8] E.g.: Raffaele Garucci, Storia dell arte christiana, Prato, 1876. N. Kondakoff, Hist. d.l'art Byz., Paris, 1882.

[9] Die Wiener Genesis, herausgegeben von W. v. Hartel u. F. Wickhoff. *Beilage z. XV. u. XVI. B. d. Jahrb. d. kunsthist. Sammlungen d. A. H. Kaiserhauses, Vienna, 1895.* Reprinted: F. Wickhoff, Römische Kunst, Vienna, 1912. Translated: Mrs S. A. Strong, Roman Art, London, 1900.

[10] A. Haseloff, Codex purpureus Rossanensis. Die Miniaturen der Evangelienhandschrift von Rossano, Berlin, 1898, stresses the connection between both manuscripts and attributes them to the second half of the VII Century or later.

[11] A. Baumstark, Bild u. Liturgie im antiochenischen Evangelienbuchschmuck d. VI. Jahrhunderts, *Ehrengabe deutscher Wissenschaft für Johann Georg Herzog v. Sachsen, Freiburg in Br., 1920.*

[12] A. Grabar, Les peintures de l'évangéliaire de Sinope, Paris, 1948. A comparison of the three manuscripts with the famous manuscript in the Laurentiana in Florence written in Syriac by the monk Rabulas in the monastery of Zagba in Mesopotamia in 586 shows a far less intimate relationship.

[13] P. Buberl, Das Problem d. Wiener Genesis, *Jahrb. d. kunsthist. Sammlungen in Wien N.F.X., 1936.* Idem, Die Wiener Genesis, *Beschreibendes Verzeichnis d. illuminierten Handschriften in Osterreich, VIII, 4, 1937.*

[14] Th. Birt, Die Buchrolle in d. Kunst, Leipzig, 1907. K. Lehmann Hartleben, Die Trajanssäule, Berlin, 1926, refutes this theory mainly on the ground that the scenes appear not to illustrate any known text but to be invented for the purpose of decorating that particular triumphal monument.

[15] K. Weitzmann, The Joshua Roll, Princeton, 1948, is a detailed monograph on the subject.

[16] Cod. lat. 3225 (Vatican Virgil); Cod. lat. 3867 (Virgilius Romanus), also in the Vatican, is considered to be either of a later date or else to reflect some provincial stylistic idiosyncrasies. Cf. C. Nordenfalk, Great Centuries of Painting II, Book Illustration, Skira, 1957.

[17] Cod. F. 205 inf.—R. Bianchi Bandinelli, Hellenistic Byzantine Miniatures of the Iliad, Olten, 1955, assigns the actual manuscript to the end of the V, or even to the VI Century, regarding it as a compilation which includes copies of III-Century prototypes, similar to the 'Flood' (our Pl. 1).

[18] Notes on East Christian Miniatures, *The Art Bulletin XI, New York, 1929.*

[19] Illustrations in Roll and Codex, a study of the origin and method of text illustration, Princeton, 1947.

[20] C. H. Kraeling, The Synagogue. The Excavations at Dura-Europos, Final Report VIII, Part I.

[21] K. Weitzmann, Die Illustrationen d. Septuaginta, *Münchner Jahrb. d. bild. Kunst. 3. Ser. III/IV, 1952/3.* He finds, e.g., the similarity between the Creation of Adam in the Cotton Bible and the Creation of Man by Prometheus on ancient sarcophagi so striking that the existence of a common archetype, i.e. an illustration in a classical mythological manuscript, must be assumed.

[22] A. Grabar, Le thème rel. d. fresques d. l. synagogue d. Doura, *Revue d. l'hist. d. religions CXXII/CXXIV, 1941/42.*

[23] Weitzmann, loc. cit.—C. O. Nordström, Some Jewish Legends in Byzant. Art (with bibliography), *Byzantion, XV/X XXVII, 1955/57.* O. Pächt kindly drew my attention to this article.

[24] C. O. Nordström, Spätjüdische Reminiszenzen i.d. altchristl. u. byzant. Kunst, *Actes du X. Congr. intern. d'Etudes byzant., 1955, Istanbul, 1957.*

[25] J. and O. Pächt, An unknown Cycle of Illustrations of the Life of Joseph, *Cahiers archéologiques VII, Paris, 1954.*